ON SUMMER SOLSTICE ROAD

Jerry Garcia

Green Tara Press

Los Angeles

2016

ACKNOWLEDGEMENTS

Thank you to the editors of the following journals and anthologies in which several of these poems have appeared in earlier forms.

Askew Poetry Journal, Chiron Review, Lummox, San Pedro River Review, Cultural Weekly, poeticdiversity, Wide Awake: Poets of Los Angeles and Beyond (Beyond Baroque), Alternate Lanes: An Anthology of Travel (Sybaritic Press, 2012) *Valley Contemporary Poets Anthology* 2010 (VCP Press), *The Coiled Serpent: Poets Arising from the Cultural Quakes and Shifts of Los Angeles* (*Tia Chucha's Press*)

Appreciation and praise to Laurel Ann Bogen and Michael C Ford for their continual support and guidance. Special thanks to Robert Krut, liz gonzález and Nancy-Jean Pément for kind words and coffee. Thank you, also, Douglas Richardson for the punctuation. Special gratitude to the awesome Becky Garcia who allows me time and space for poetry in our lives together.

Cover Art: *Los Angeles Union Station with Freeway Mural by Frank Romero* photographed and edited by Jerry Garcia. www.gratefulnotdead.com

Author Portrait: David Palmer www.davidpalmerimages.com
Book Design: Andrea Reider

Green Tara Press
Los Angeles, CA
www.greentarapress.com

MORE PRAISE FOR *ON SUMMER SOLSTICE ROAD*

Jerry Garcia's poems are fully situated in time and place, and in the liminal spaces of emergent identity. Set against the backdrop of the City of Angels, these poems offer snapshots of the evolving self. This work will resonate with anyone who has wondered who they are meant to be in the world. Readers will find a brother, a friend, a kindred spirit in each piece.

DR. NANCY-JEAN PÉMENT, Ventura County Arts Council

Jerry Garcia's wonderful On Summer Solstice Road starts in the streets of Los Angeles, and goes onto to show us that city from countless angles. What makes this book special is the way this start expands out to take us through all of California, and beyond to the larger scope of American history. These are poems filled with vivid imagery and evocative ideas, all the stronger for the warmth beneath them. These are poems about a city, and a country, but filled with heart.

ROBERT KRUT, Poet, *This Is the Ocean*

On Summer Solstice Road is a compelling, resonant collection of poems. Jerry Garcia takes us on a cruise through his Los Angeles. Guitar music plays on the radio while profound images roll across the pages—a brown-skinned mother "incessantly" scrubs and polishes her copper to keep it from turning green like the steeple at Bullock's Wilshire and "a Del Taco wrapper floats over suburban lawns." Car models evolve, and males grow from a Catholic schoolboy, "harangued by adult fears" and shunned by a girl, into "mustachioed men" who snort coke and drive drunk. The city also transforms—a boy's friends disappear when his neighborhood is demolished to build Interstate 60, and "generations of concrete bury that old green field" on "3rd and Fairfax." But hope revs the engine forward. Kick back and enjoy the ride.

liz gonzález, poet, writer, and
director of Uptown Word & Arts

Garcia's work at its most linear is, certainly, emanating from the poetic imagination, but appears more qualified as autobiographic interludes viewed in the ragged vertical tradition. With a bitter glitter of city-dweller intensity, he eschews the suspect poems of sunset over seascape manic-depressions and becomes a firebrand observer of urban grit.

MICHAEL C FORD, poet, playwright
and Grammy-Nominated recording artist

TABLE OF CONTENTS

I. EXPOSITION

96 Minutes on the Clock Tower   3
There Will Be No Fiesta Today   6
At The Grove   7
Music Hall Comedian   9
Monsoon Skyline   11
Valet Parking at the Ganja House   12
Suburban Recessional   13
Epoch of Analog   14
Troponin of Protest   15
December 14, 2012   16
Building a Nation Pantoum   17
War Without My Heroes   18
Patina   20

II. CONTEXT

Blaring Summer Skies Take Silence as Mood, Not Dreams   23
The Great Western Fair   25
500 Miles   26
American History 1962   27
Lupe   28
A Summer Day at the Atlantic Square   32
Benediction   34
A Guitar Covers His Desire   36
Top Gun Mythology   38
Other Angels   39
Pochismo Me   41
Los Muertos   43
The Truth of Clutter   45
Interstate 60   47

III. PASSAGE

America   51
On Summer Solstice Road   52
Salt   54
Oh Montana de Oro   56
On Persephone's Travel Day   58
Toward the PCH of Divinity in the 1970s   59
Insulation   62
Time Passage Illumination   65
Spring   67
Horror Show at the 99-Cent Bijou   68
Debit/Credit   70
Window Strikes   71
Plastic Bottle Vodka   72
Memory Preserved in a Blue Ceramic Ashtray   73
The Last Sitting   75
Father's Day   76

IV. REENTRY

Dark Swirling Sky Shadows a Worn-Out Barn on an
    Untried Road   79
California June Gloom: In Dakota They Wait for Weather   80
Re-Entry   82
While Walking the Dog Last Evening   83
Once a Frozen Landscape   84
I Am Waiting   85
Lexicon   86
In Case of Criticism   87
The Highway Is a Breeze, the Forest Is a Cave   88
Just Before Dawn   89
Three Holiday Stars   90
How to Bury Your Dad   91

FOR GUS GARCIA

1. EXPOSITION

"A new nation does not write poetry."

96 MINUTES
ON THE
CLOCK TOWER

I wander through these blackened ruins
thinking that nobody has ever made proper use of murder.
KENNETH PATCHEN

Hot August 1966
bullets ring like
nickels on concrete
and echo a life's value,
five cents on the dollar.

Charles Whitman takes
what newspapers call
"the unassailable"
clock tower advantage
—impossible to challenge.

The flip side
of the suicide coin
is murder.

For ninety-six minutes
Whitman sniped at people
he didn't even care to know
and foretold new trends
of American violence:
Harris and Klebold
of Columbine, Cho
in Blacksburg, James
Eagen Holmes
of Aurora, Colorado,
twenty children slaughtered

at Sandyhook Elementary School,
forty-nine proud revelers
in Orlando, Florida.

The mid-sixties rapid-change world
was not equipped
for the bullet parade
of Whitman's new brand
of shock.

Summer classes,
campus bustle,
tinny radio transistors
full of *Yellow Submarine*
and Lovin' Spoonful
songs that played well
with the heat.
Not since medieval times
had public bloodshed
been as commonplace.

High-caliber
like the Kennedy gun
where a President's blood
had some probability
of a reason.
Now televised mad snipers
shoot your neighbor's kids
on university concrete,
on the high school campus,
in movie theaters
in nightclubs meant
for dancing.

Eden's National Enquirer calls
Whitman the first
*high-speed freeway-chasing
postal rage sensationalist.*

Headlines for the ages.

The flip side of the
suicide coin
is murder.

Charles Whitman ripped
his mother's skin
and murdered his wife in bed;
then offered the insurance policy
of his own death
as redemption
for a tortured mind.

In the ninety-sixth minute,
deputies Martinez and McCoy
challenged Whitman's unassailable
clock-tower advantage
and flipped his coin
along with our perceptions
of anger and despondency.

The flip side
of the murder coin
is suicide.

THERE WILL BE NO FIESTA TODAY

A POEM FOR RUBEN SALAZAR

Tank treads flatten papier-mâché,
caramel sticks crepe to asphalt.

    There will be no fiesta today.

On a tear-gas-emptied street,
shards and casings litter curbs.
        Missiles fly through
            the Silver Dollar doorway.

With feigned expressions of grief
we turn our heads from a haze
      that suffocates the coherent voice.

In large-screen living rooms
new carpet and designer wares
    co-opt rubber bullets and batons.

A Del Taco wrapper floats
       over suburban lawns
but no one sees the real mess we've made.

We pull the shades closed
and thank God for our safety.

Shamelessly, we exchange masa for flour.

AT THE GROVE

Ghosts sell produce
from the backs of Studebakers,
phantom children race miniature cars
like it was 1954
on the asphalt parking lot
covering what's left
of its former track

on 3rd and Fairfax in Los Angeles.
Fountains boogie onto cobblestones,
it's like Vegas with a trolley car.

Land of Gilmore!
Where Earl Gilmore displayed
the famous "Red Lion" logo of self-pump
 "Gas-a-terias"

Home to L.A. baseball
—The Hollywood Stars,
the available team,
the team you saw with your older brother.

I strain to hear
the crack of runs batted in,
whistles and shrill of public address
announcer's roar "… it's outta here"
umpire barking
"Safe!"

But generations of concrete
bury that old green field,
consumers lurch from
parking structures
to a pretend main street
of corporate coffee houses
and Oprah's book club
where mimes and security guards
smother memories.

As dizzied surround-sound movie-goers
disgorge the multi-plex
I shake my head—
not the old drive-in theater
not where families hid under blankets
to avoid additional charge,
not where teenagers groped their first sex
not little racers burning up the tracks
not ball players sliding through innings.

Now it's children sliding past frames of lingerie,
designer Hawaiian shirts and Cubic Zirconium.
They look for glittered gumballs and new electronic controls.

I look for passage back through maintenance access
and service alleys
seeking that forgotten field of summer play
past the parking lot produce
and lanky players that stretch and glide
for the little guys with dirty faces
to cheer and play their maracas of Cracker Jack boxes.

Kids and visitors do not hear those echoes,
smoking immigrant dishwashers
frown at off-tune Karaoke singers
and I glare at my daughter's cotton candy smile.

I wonder why she calls this a good time.

MUSIC HALL COMEDIAN

FOR JOHNNY CARSON

The drummer's
burlesque rim shot
splatters over
bored anxious coughs
and wheezing
from behind footlight faces
on musty seats
the audience waits
for my jaws to stop their banter
they wait for the girl
with the jewels on top
who promenades
draped silk hanging like curtain slivers
pretending to hide
her pasty-covered nipples.

Carita deLovely
with her many veils
glows and struts
into my bit:
seltzer bottle
wilted daisy
Harpo horn
and baggy pants.
(They all retreat stage left
forgetting to wait for the blackout.)

She dips and fans
smiles and pirouettes
dances bemused
someone always yells
"take it off"
but it's strip Tease
she never disrobes
until pounding

raw music power
canned heavy metal
banging rock 'n' roll
from subwoofers
scores the scene.

Blue light shadows
red light mirrors

Then Tiffany takes her stage
white light overexposes flesh
naked flesh
tanned unblemished flesh
oiled and sequined flesh
pierced bellybutton flesh.
No one yells "take it off"
there's nothing to take off.

A modern tailored Siren
she twirls the pole
cartwheels and dives
springs off the stage
lands light as a kitten.

She's on her back
she's in your face
it's gynecology night
in the Gentlemen's Lair.

When the stage lights dim
the house lights glare
I haul my baggy pants
and sagging bladder home
where I watch a new comedy star
insult my TV screen
and wonder:

Can I ever be funny again?

MONSOON SKYLINE

Midnight thunderhead
hovers above vertical bar graph
of metropolitan halation.
Sealed patina framed windows
throw random blue sparks
on foot-stepped puddles.

Hooded valets lock rusted gates,
trip on Coke cans down to the Metro;
café wait-staff turns chairs over tables,
journeyman lawyers aim corporate sedans
to vacate downtown perspiration.
Delivery truck spritz pavement,
lost tourist makes U-turn
on one-way street,
electric drizzle descends
like a drawn-curtain fade-out
muffling the booms of Bald Mountain.

Dawn's alabaster lamplight
creates steaming silhouettes
of bicycles and shopping carts;
morning guards don lapels
while last night's security takes a walk.

Friday morning's
Jack Purcell traffic jam
emerges from the 7th Street/Metro Station
to invade the valley of worn itinerants.
Just another soggy-pavement day
unusually cool to the touch.

VALET PARKING AT THE GANJA HOUSE

Pot used to be difficult,
like an "A" in science class
or a social studies report
about dark alleys and tenements.
It was strangely coded phone calls
to ne'er-do-well friends,
flakey observers of life
behind the bleachers
playing guitar out of tune
and off beat to the school bell

Marijuana was danger,
a night in the hoosegow,
for a baggie of rip-off oregano.
Boo was for cleverly hiding
in your well-bunkered bedroom;
wet towels on the threshold,
an over-spray of cologne,
Glade or talcum powder.

Now with a script,
a trip to the strip mall
will cool your Jones.
A freebie walk past Officer Ray.
Edible, odorless.
Drive-thru, valet parking,
credit cards.

Oh man, just driving by
gives me the munchies.

SUBURBAN RECESSIONAL

Men dressed like funerals
emerge from evergreen hedges
to outfit jacaranda trees in black tie.
Cats herd onto sidewalks singing *In Paridisum*,
children float Popsicle-stick rafts
in gutter-water streams.
Palm fronds bow like acolytes
to wrinkled elders pushing shopping carts.
Barbecues create multiple plumes of suburban incense
as crows chorus benediction.

Clouds are cirrus and loose,
jet condensation tracks blue spaces,
shadows make the sign of the cross
on upswept sidewalks.
Nuns pray in blue wardrobe
on every street corner.
The mailman passes with the redemption
of John the Baptist along the way
to losing his head.

EPOCH OF ANALOG

Oh, howl young lovers,
orgasm discreetly muffled
under pillows of
"love me tender" sex,
vacuum tube high fidelity sex,
backseat Chevy sex.

The Epoch of Analog
ends with a cipher,
buried in
signal-to-noise high-frequency hiss,
crackles and pops
on vinyl strands,
diamond needles
scratch.

Now, by glow
of Liquid Crystal Displays,
hot-swappable fucking
comes in bit-rates,
podcast screenings every 20 minutes,
sampled lover shrieks
compressed to megabytes,
lost in the ether
and replaced
by a simple
download.

TROPONIN OF PROTEST

A protein within a troponin complex helps regulate the
heartbeat and can be used as an indicator of myocardial
infarction (heart attack).

Mind set:
accrual of uncertainty
blindly coursing
days.

Resuscitation.

Roadblocks
hold back light
like dementia.
Temptation closes
callous arteries
of dilemma
looking for fault.

Resuscitation.

Volcanic road rage
revolts against the destitute.
Thrombotic ankles drag
like screaming
canyons
on fire.

Resuscitation
nil.

DECEMBER 14, 2012

Cloud shadowed day
absorbs light
from scrubbed faces.

Impending rain
won't wash
sanguine flesh
from violations
of pounding lead.

Dark hail
tears up
young dreams
and purpose.

BUILDING A NATION PANTOUM

A new nation does not write poetry;
it establishes borders.
A new nation does not create opera;
it builds an army.

A new nation establishes borders.
Pondering preservation,
it builds an army
and mines resources.

Pondering preservation,
a new nation creates orders of law
and mines resources
while birthing children.

A new nation creates orders of law.
It builds bridges and levees
while birthing children
and planning for disaster.

A new nation builds bridges and levees.
It bargains for business
and plans for disaster.
It alphabetizes, counts, and stockpiles.

Bargaining for business,
a new nation does not create opera.
It alphabetizes, counts, and stockpiles.
A new nation does not write poetry.

WAR WITHOUT MY HEROES

Wake up, Diane Arbus.
The world needs your photographs:
      amputee soldiers
      beheaded corpses
      anguished mothers.

Margaret Bourke-White,
we need your pictures too.
      GI's pass out candy bars
      against a backdrop of torn burqas
      and shattered mosques.

No one can *See It Now*
Edward R. Murrow.
      No one can see the truth.
      Our daily news
      is a show of pixels
     —discreet elements scattered
      into our living rooms
      to paint reaction.

Sylvia Plath, please
take another breath!
We are all suffocating
from global depression.

William Butler Yeats.
The time has come,
        your falcon singes his wings
        in its *widening gyre.*

Prophets, poets,
truth-tellers of our time,
unheard and vexed,
voices hidden.

Even your belief in love
is stifled, John Lennon.

    All you need.

PATINA

They were called
    hoity-toity
the gilded shoppers
at Bullocks Wilshire,
the uptown department store
of Los Angeles lore.

Its copper tower had turned green.
As a child
I never understood why.
It was supposed to be
shiny copper orange,
like mother's
bathroom doorknobs,
like everything in her house

incessantly scrubbed and polished.
She strived to keep her copper
orange and shiny;
would not let the metal skin
corrode like the classic green steeple
on the art deco of L.A.'s retail icon.

Patina-removing,
I later learned, is detrimental
to claims of authenticity.

2. CONTEXT

"That is when I understood the holy water."

BLARING SUMMER SKIES
TAKE SILENCE AS MOOD,
NOT DREAMS

We piled into brother Joe's
'57 Bel Air,
Sea Foam and chrome,
two-toned with white fins.
Vinyl seats, fluffy dice.
A large steering wheel
counterturned to the boulevard
away from our house and its
white calla lily hedge,
its finely edged
lawn.

Green like Easter,
straw swayed
along the roadside
in vacant lots
of abandonment
and undermined growth.

We drove 27.8 miles
to the San Fernando Mission.
Parked among pilgrim cars
pitted by dead gnats of travel.
Quietly entering adobe brick,
mother put a white-lace doily
on her head
sprinkled me with water
from the fount of sinners
and asked God to bless
her gloomy child.

Then she supplicated
on cold stone
at the altar
of Junipero Serra.

Beeswax and shellac
touched my senses
like a sneeze
while the mission bells
tolled redemption.

Through funnels of light
dust motes fell.
A fidgeting boy in short pants
pointed a Michelangelo finger
and called me
the devil.

When it was time to go in peace,
we left under a roost of pigeons
begging from terracotta tiles.
I saw that boy stumble
and scrape his knee
on jagged mission rock.
Wings fluttered
with a turbulence foreign
to the everyday repentant
in Sunday go-to-meeting clothes.

When I laughed, the boy showed
real tears and a crow cawed disharmony.

That is when I understood
the holy water.

THE GREAT WESTERN FAIR

Most had never seen cows,
touched a penned up swine,
nor smelled the organic bouquet
of rural life.

A yellow-bus ride
to the traveling country fair
unlocked the minds
of uninitiated nine-year-olds
far from their city limits.

Among the flying flags, costumed guides,
and asphalt covered by green hay,
the animals looked kind,
though shackled, in chain link cages.

500 MILES

After Peter, Paul & Mary

The sandman stirs
through the shadowed clutter
of my bedroom
on a school night
in November 1963
when the double bass notes
of Dick Kniss
major into my
reverie.

My brother Lou,
just home from the college library,
sits in the tungsten wash
of our family den;
11pm feels like dawn,
subsonic notes resonate
from the Magnavox.

It's a profound,
nevertheless, mellow walk
through silhouette branches
of guitar strides and harmony;
the night becomes ethereal
when Mary Travers' voice
arcs my bedroom
like Tinker Bell.

AMERICAN HISTORY 1962

The war Cold
the enemy Red
our parochial uniforms Blue.

When Sister Margaret clapped
we dove beneath
our pencil-scribed
school desks;
the bombs would
soon be launched,
seconds to impact
moments for prayer,
the plaster of Paris Virgin Mary
blessed the panicky believers
cherub faces pushed onto linoleum
to protect innocent eyes
from flashing waves of reprisal,
air-raid sirens shrilled in training.

We were seven-years-old,
harangued by adult fears
about bomb shelters and Armageddon.
Walking home from school,
corduroy pants itched,
leather soles wore thin on hot concrete,
transistor radio earplugs filled our heads
with scratchy news radio.

LUPE

I.

Named for
La Virgen de Guadalupe,
by age thirteen
comparisons to the Virgin Mother
are dubious.

It is June 1968,
our last day spent together
in grade school.
Lupe leads me
to the overgrown bushes
of her rundown backyard.

The Peter Pan blouse
of her parochial school uniform
unbuttons,
her JC Penny brassiere
unfastens to reveal
sepia-toned flesh
and purple nipples.
Doe-eyed and pretty,
she encourages me to touch.

Trembling hands hesitate,
anticipation becomes
a wet spot on blue corduroy.
Lupe's eyes close with disdain
she reassembles
into her honor student veneer
and leaves me in her backyard
alone.

Skulking home,
Santa Ana winds groan embarrassed voices
of disappointment,
snickering at lost expectations,
failure and shame.

II.

Summer becomes a restless collection
of baseball cards and balsa wood airplanes
chewing gum and skateboards,
Gomer Pyle on the television
and rock n' roll on the transistor.

I try not to think about Lupe.
But when I find my brother's stash
of *Playboy* magazines
I realize a new education,
part fable, part science,
not at all like Sister Mary Margaret's
Catechism.

Ready to revisit Lupe
and her garden's overgrowth
I ride my Sears Stingray bike to her
dry-weed neighborhood.

III.

Lupe sits alone on her father's broken porch
wearing pancake makeup,
eyeliner and killer mascara.

I cut circles and wheelies
on her sidewalk, summoning
the necessary courage to say hello.

Lupe rises, poised and confident,
tall in borrowed high heels,
her chin tilts in the pose
of an Aztec Princess.
Her silk blouse reveals
push-up outlines of teenage breasts.

In slow motion
her dark eyes and glossy lips
come toward me.
The warm wind carries the sounds
of distant children at play
a distant radio distorts
Brown Eyed Girl.

Lupe saunters within reach,
the adult aroma of perfume
and the sweetness of her
glossy smile overcome
my bicycle balance.
I stumble and grab
the handle bars
as she passes by,
I can only gaze.

IV.

Tire squeals and the booming
rhythm of a 440 Chevy Camaro's idle
break into my daydream.

Muscle-bound, high school senior Antonio
opens the door
Lupe gracefully takes her seat
her nyloned leg slides over the tuck-n-roll.

Sitting on my banana-seat,
sniffling in torn jeans and dusty Keds,
I wonder "How did Lupe become
so much older?"

"When did I become invisible?"

A SUMMER DAY AT THE ATLANTIC SQUARE

Humid, wilting palm tree weather
sticky Popsicle spill on sidewalk sparkle
Saturday afternoon pilgrimage
to the local top 40 record stand.

Single earplug transistor radio
broadcasts Bob, *the Hullabalooer,*
into my right ear.
In the left ear, a ballpark cheers.
Don Drysdale toes rubber on an RCA color TV
in the Singer appliance store display.
Beatles sing *Lady Madonna*
through bases loaded, no R.B.I. innings.
Sunburned fans get antsy on the tube.
Radio plays Felix Chevrolet commercials.
The *Big D* throws another whiff
the side retires
while the Byrds *Turn, Turn, Turn;*
David Crosby harmonizing Pete Seeger lyrics
over McGuinn's 12-string jangle.
Pennant-winning talent!

Summer boys pouring from winner's dugout.
A sweet harmonica betrays the blues
making Stevie Wonder
the Jackie Robinson of AM radio.
Postgame channel-switching
American Bandstand
Dick Clark standing on the mound
music livens both ears,
salted nuts and ERA
in trade for 45 rpms.

Music vs. baseball
a doubleheader for sure.
This odd music-driven adolescent
joins that legion of teenage boys
who invented air guitar,
pretending to choke
a rosewood guitar neck
like a Louisville Slugger.

BENEDICTION

Tantum Ergo is the last two stanzas from the Eucharistic Hymn (Pange Lingua) which is sung during the Benediction of the Blessed Sacrament in the Catholic Church. It was composed by St. Thomas Aquinas.

Under yellow plaster
of SoCal imitation adobe
children tenors intone

Down in adoration falling,

Burning candles and incense
waft over lacquered pews of pine

Lo! the sacred Host we hail.

Sweating late to Benediction
I loudly jostle the noisy push-bar entry
the church door clunks and echoes

Lo! o'er ancient forms departing,

My reefer-scented shirt glows purple
pungent odor trails my entrance

Newer rites of grace prevail.

Side-stepping Sister Margaret Mary's glare
kneelers bang pews as I squeeze
through snickering blue-and-white classmates

Faith for all defects supplying,

Gray-suited men pass wicker baskets
collecting coins and dollars
in the purple stained-glass glow of saintly lives.

Where the feeble senses fail. Amen.

A GUITAR COVERS HIS DESIRE

Her to-the-ass
generation defining
hair swayed with hips
and faded blue jeans
as she sauntered the hallways
of mid-city high school.
Joey's head turned to his locker,
he was too much the nerd to speak,
too scared to touch
the *Rock n Roll Woman*
whose dark eyes stared
directly at him.

Though he yearned
to feel up the woven hemp
of her hippie blouse;
Joey imagined how
he would lightly brush
her velvet mini-skirt
with his guitar fingering hand.
But he refrained from any attempt
to glide along her lithe
brown skin.

Joey couldn't do this on his own.
He excused fear
with green-glass jug wine
and anti-social stares.
Grasping at joints to loosen
the tightly wound nylon and brass
of youth.

Spring was cruel.
She ran freely though the grass,
kissing the older boys behind bushes,
reappearing flushed and sweaty.
Joey played at being Neil Young,
aloof, off camera gaze;
guitar covering his desire,

he unwittingly sang
blessings for her free spirit
while cursing his own
unintended virtue.

TOP GUN MYTHOLOGY

DAEDALUS & ICARUS

Daedalus touched down at the drive-in
for a burger, shake and fries.
Skating waitresses looked askance
as he begged slick son Icarus
to make good use of his feathers.

The guys jeered their waxed up friend
as he obediently flapped his wings
to follow father's departure.
Soon, like Maverick against Viper,
Icarus soared past cruising altitude.

Daedalus flew steady.
Icarus climbed and rotated
Top Gunning his way
to the stars.

Dad wished Icarus were more concerned
about safety than looking cool.
"Where are you going, Son?"
"Just one more high, Dad!" Icarus shouted
as he climbed toward the searing sun.

Daedalus didn't curse
his plummeting son's arrogance;
after all, he had given the boy his wings.

OTHER ANGELS

Wings shoot from
my shoulder blades.
I glide over ocean mist
and touch down on
a cloud.

I thought
I would see angels,
other angels.

Perhaps the girl knew
she would shatter first.
As I tumble
through thick air
I see my young lover
smack the sand
and rock below.
Arms flail
fingers crack
gritty surf covers
her with a pall
of seaweed.

I plummet
to her side,
—no wings sprout
—no parachute pulls my reprieve
—no zephyr sweeps me to Heaven.

Air and surf
flutter static
through my ears.
I open my mouth
to bitter salt,
look into wet sand,

and become
a seagull's

last
screech.

POCHISMO ME

WITH NO APOLOGIES TO EDWARD JAMES OLMOS

Far from a serape
or colored bandanas,
my mother feared
I would be scorned
because her skin was brown.
So she conjured
a white child.

In the parochial
neighborhood of
her mind
I spoke English,
dressed in houndstooth
and corduroy,
chanted Latin and
incensed altars
of a conqueror church
to rise above those
who would look like her.

I whet appetites for salsa
in the lacy bedrooms of
pale skinned princesses,
while big-ten firms placed me
on their employee rosters.

Invited into their mansions
they use the word "Hispanic"
because "Mexican"
was thought to be impolite.
But in the Barrio I am just Pocho,
a Coconut, some think sell out.

It is true that I enjoy driving a *BMW*
over the fabled *Chevy*.
I'll take Sushi over a burrito.
I fuck blondes not Latinas.

This skin is not *Coppertone:*
I was born in East L.A.
and stand, bewildered yet proud,
on this divide
with my mother's color on my arms,
and her fears in my heart.

LOS MUERTOS

Resplendently rotted flesh,
calcified bones,
exacerbate
my reluctance
to participate
in a life swollen
from
passing time's
venom.

Wooden skulls
unhinge and laugh
at passing frailty.

My dead ones
promenade with me
through trellised streets
where crutches, canes
and yards of electrocardiograms
hang like discards at Lourdes,
where pilgrims pray
for temporal well being.

This arthritic knuckle
knows my grandfather's pain.
Alcohol confuses my head
weakening organs
like the disease
of my brother's judgment.

While counting
falling strands
of receding
hairline,
my arteries clog
and I become the curse
of my dead father
holding the Crucifix
to a defiant son.

So let the music play.

THE TRUTH OF CLUTTER

From willowed streets
dirty breezes track
remnants and soil;
through crumbled foyer
reverent steps ponder
a musty-air predicament.

Light-leaking curtains shadow
ripped-carpet terrain,
ghostly plaster-of-paris statues
and patinas of dusty icons
crowd this house
like a Salvation Army thrift store.

Boxes loom eight feet high:
brown corrugations,
white and smooth,
full of logos,
Tiffany
Florsheim
and *Bekins*
mildewed, stained and torn
—a risky house of cards.

Perhaps something
like the Grail hides
among the torn and yellowed wallpaper
where light abandons
a grandfather's struggle with time.

In a far-reached 10-by-10 room,
too far for any voice to carry,
overflowing mahogany armoires
overshadow a failed four-poster.

Down groaning steps
floorboards sweat mildew
concrete basement smells
like industrial rubber
and rodent droppings.

Could these be
stepping stones
to the gates of Hell?

Twenty-two sealed boxes,
a wooden apple crate,
disassembled lawnmower parts
and other peculiar relics.

What could be next?
Wading through diffused memory
gray matter falls
like resurrection dust.

Furniture crashes
like thunderbolts
like evil entrance
like howling fears
like a curse thrown upon
unsuspecting shoulders

a last memory
a gripped hammer
an agonizing squeeze of the heart
scattered brads
on a workbench

a splendid
awe-inspired gaze
into the truth of clutter.

INTERSTATE 60

I saw my neighborhood destroyed by destiny, when I was six years old.
My friends disappeared for life, reduced to the fine powder of
    demolition.
I watched their houses splintered and smashed to host an eight-lane
    highway.

I played with the long boards, the broken porcelain of sinks and
    toilets, cinder block perimeters, cracked foundations, silt and rusty
    pipes when water no longer flowed from the homes of childhood
    friends.

Baseball cards and jacks covered by weeds, toys traded for rock piles,
    chain-link fences, bulldozers and cranes.
Mortar applied, covered by black sticky asphalt, the bitter odor that
    permeated the nights of my youth.

The freeway emerged, surf and gulls in the speed of traffic, squeal of
    brakes, trucks gusting a new era.
Highways separated east from north of east, the immigrant Russian
    replaced by the middle-class Mexican-American replaced by new
    immigrant Chinese.

A skinny sixteen-year-old boy stared through concrete pylons.
Boisterous pals, cigars and joints, became the interior of a teenage
    night.
Heading west to music, tie-dye and unwashed hair, smoking and
    spilling wine on the roots buried underneath that freeway.

Ocean waves head like schooners of beer, a blue yacht background to
    the destitute of Main Street the homeless disappeared or wished
    they had.
99 cent movie halls collapsed, apartments and vendor shacks flattened
    to make way for malls of fast food and plastic fashion.

Streets square and parallel like an engineer's grid, but I cannot drive
    straight.
Noise in my head pierces sharper than squealing traffic, louder than
    the motor's torque.
I must shift gears and exit this junkie-fueled existence before I too
    disappear.

Freeways don't cross cemeteries, they swerve around.
Under a concrete street bridge, throat dry, breath caught as if my last, I
    purge fear of the miles ahead and reach to rev my engine forward
    on this sprawling Western highway.

3. PASSAGE

"We look for a better horizon."

AMERICA
With no apology to Allen Ginsberg

America, I may not be Allen Ginsberg, but I am the incongruity within your borders, clay eroding from plodding footsteps and battered domesticity; mothers ignoring talent off-springing with dreaded pop culture, verve that could not be controlled, dressed in corduroy, saluting flags, dropping under desks to the solipsism of industrial giants.

America, I don't want to fuck you. I don't want to graffiti your road signs, oil your beaches, wretch in your alleys, tea-bag your faith. I fear to bleed your veterans, disregard your children, hide your Mexicans. Arms too short to reach the radio, I cannot tune out whimpering static upheavals. Tires bumping road dividers from the boring rhetoric of duplicity.

America, I degrade over the Guthrie highway, dirt roads and mottled bridges, I fight on the golf courses and tarmacs of your flat-lands, on the crumbling rocks of your mountains, the infested waters of your boundaries, in clean lakes reflecting skyscrapers of corruption. On the air mattress of simplicity, tones and half-notes resonate from bird-dropping on your grandeur.

America, magnificent lightning storms flash the retinas of my flight through paleo-rock and mixed-grass prairie, deeply gazing into your stripes of creation; pink layered mineral-rust etches granite so old that my birth will seemingly never come.

ON SUMMER SOLSTICE ROAD

We beg the air for moisture,
drink bottled rations promised
          to the next mile
and try to soothe the grief
of scorched limbs, blistered feet.

Sandblasted panoramas
degrading paths
and broken posts
discourage our journey.

Sage wilts   cactus stoops
                    power lines corrode
                         humor fails

The wheeze grows heavy
                    our vision strains
knees seize like rusting gates
sheer sand dunes snicker
          at the chaos.

Sweat, may as well be blood,
streaks on rocks and bones
artifacts crushed to gravel
by the heavy-footed compression
of many generations.

We look for a better horizon
but nothing protects us
from the unforgiving greed
of a prolonged summering sun.

We rupture and collapse
from futile attempts
to rebuild our dried-out oasis.

Not even the stalwart yucca stands a chance
against quixotic winds
from what might be giants.

SALT

I canter through
    the roiling gray

    head lost

in low-lying clouds
of morning's dread
      vapor

heavy wheels roll
the leaden gates
that hold back
      Hell's blaze

Perspiration mottles my forehead

Like garden hoses
ready to spurt
    nerves quiver

    without enough pressure
to appease impending doom

Walking backwards
only takes me closer
    to the original sin

I reach for my ankles
    but still cannot see my feet

Night sweats dampen
    head to toe
    saturating jockey shorts
    and one-thousand-thread-count
        linen

Hey, send in a crew to mine this bedroom!

Precious minerals are being expended
        here!

OH MONTAÑA DE ORO

Your orange slate
                    juts

        to salute the Pacific

A young woman
            stiff as a Naval Lieutenant

            faces tealed   waves

                breathes   seaweed
                    scented foam

No photograph could explain the day's
                        state of mind.

            Children drag firewood

                        hikers rest against your weedy
                                        bluff

            She cleanses herself with salt water
                    balances bare feet on broken rocks
                        with ballerina poise

The setting sun competes with your amber cliffs

        Your beach empties of tourists

                        rests

Even pelicans seek shelter

Removing her green knit sweater
    exposing bone white breasts
        to briny cold

She stretches her lanky body to the sea

        like a dare

The un-credited female
        commits adultery

            with shells and sand
                crabs

        on the stained shore

of your golden

        California.

ON PERSEPHONE'S TRAVEL DAY

When I awoke this morning, my eyes freely opened.

The sun had evaporated the gray swirls of shipwreck dreams
     that usually precede my day.

I whistled into the shaving mirror, and the shower
     stayed hot through my ablutions.

The city traffic had been dismissed.
     I did not spill coffee on my shirt.

The phones did not ring.
My heart did not stop.

Oh Gods' due praise and Gods who damn
preserve this day in the Bulfinch of my life!

For surely the Hell that froze over today
     will have thawed by the time I wake tomorrow.

TOWARD THE PCH OF DIVINITY
IN THE 1970S

We found ourselves
in a *Dodge Dart* rattling
62 mph on city streets.
Jack Daniels hand over fist,
skunkweed fragranced the air,
passing headlights
punctured dilated pupils.

Four mustachioed men
in polyester prints
and double knit bell bottoms,
brothers of ethos,
following the one-night-stand circuit
of pre-infected Los Angeles.

We sauntered out The Oar House
into *Buffalo Chips*,
cross Main Street
in a chance of traffic;
nose powder glistened
in street light exposure.

At *Merlin McFly's,*
cherry-drink blondes
of college persuasion
kept an impenetrable huddle
and sent us on our way.
So we descended
upon *Big Daddy's* discotheque
like it was our right
to Travolta the floor,
a bunch of morons
with no rhythm, style
or moves.

Lights too bright,
shadows too dark
to see our own drinks.
We rabble-roused
the parking lot
and stripped gears
down Sepulveda
toward the *Wild Goose* because
the dance club was a washout.

The *Wild Goose* was a strip club
of modest means
a little bit of Vegas in Lennox, California.
Bachelor party boys
looked lost among G-strings
and pasties
while my buds
became more drunk and
extra crazy.
Davy's nosebleed
made Rorschach patterns
on his disco shirt.
Red, blue and green
stage lights triggered
one of Harvey's acid flashbacks.

Thrown out before
last call, we sat on the curb
and howled at motorists
passing on the Imperial Highway.

It took slow-paced, off-freeway maneuvers
to avoid a cop bust
and drunker than we drivers.
We snaked Sepulveda
to the Moulin Rouge
of Lincoln Blvd —*Van de Camp's*
Coffee Shop — where the waitresses
wore Dutch caps and frilly aprons
and kicked us out at dawn.

We watched sunup
from the Santa Monica Pier
hung-over and weepy
in the Hallelujah
of a fisherman's
church.

INSULATION

Oh baby, you were
so out of control,
falling out of your
dance dress
under a narcotic
summer moon.

You thought
you still had it together.

You screeched red terror.
I thought your heart
would tear open right there.
So loudly you roared
"I don't care"
and at that point I saw
the switch to your wits
shut down its current.

That's right—
you didn't care.
You didn't worry about
the confusion of uppers
or downers.

You didn't lose sleep over
thoughts of dehydration,
impending starvation.
So quickly,
like a sponge out of water
your *In Style* body
became dried flesh.

Now you sprawl on cigarette butts
and dried chewing gum
stiletto heels
awkwardly sidestep
your skeletal frame.

Counting days backwards
your lights dim,
your eyes become two hollow storerooms
insulation as thick
as the buildings around you.

Electrical conductors inert,
spark incomplete,
flashing recall:

champagne flutes
pills by the handful
cocaine lines jump-cutting
to crack pipes

and the sad faces
of former friends—
caretakers held hostage too long
by your ruin.

Ten Sunday mornings later,
corner of Cahuenga and Vine
newspaper man hawking headlines.

Drooped across cement lines
your dancewear
smudged and greasy
panty hose
shredded
caked in homeless grime,
heels busted.

Corroding like the handle
of your rusted vanity mirror
you clutch a Styrofoam cup
full of coins
from Samaritans walking
toward their redemption.

Church bells thump
in the distance.

TIME PASSAGE ILLUMINATION

1984
Hiding from sunrise
under a freeway buttress,
handkerchief soaking red,
match-burnt fingers
spill sedatives
meant to slow
a palpitating heart.

Dancing in the brazen blare
of neon nightclubs
my blonde mistress,
all cocaine thin and go-go booted,
bellies to me and laughs.

In the fluorescent basement
of my junky apartment
canvas becoming flaccid
from furious swags of dreary purples
indiscriminate strokes attempting to cover
the demanding stare
of a blank page.

The colors of Hell boiled over
and flushed away my seizing body.
In the nose-bleed aftermath,
the mistress stole my palette
and left me only umber.

2004
In my backyard swimming pool
I stare through chlorinated water
into 20 years of cross patterns.

The shadow of a telephone pole
and a crack in the cement
inexplicably remind me
of that laughing mistress.

I step through the ripples
to paint on daylight's deck
footprints dissipate
shadows change direction.

I look for the devil's art
but cannot find my palette

—not even umber.

SPRING

Leaves no room
for my dark verse.
I have no sunlit phrases for you.
Let me remain unvoiced in stagnant balmy air.

Once compatible friends,
we made a disaster of affection.
Branches backlit in baking skies
might suggest hand-holding mornings
on dewy blades of grass.

But not before damage felled the tree
like a heart attack.

HORROR SHOW

AT THE 99-CENT BIJOU

I wish I had left
you home.

Popcorn spills along
mangy aisles.
Whimpers mix
with the panic-driven
underscore of shock,
your clenched body
tears at my attention.

It is so much easier
to thrust a butcher knife
without a head buried
into my leathered sleeve.

You avert your eyes
to protect your virtue,
but I peer deeply
for more savagery.

I am the mutilator,
vengeful
bludgeoning.
I loathe your weakness,
the fluttering hand
that holds tight to my bicep.

In the distance
screams recoil,
viscera floats
in bloody waters.

Heads duck in the cold dark.
I consider the next victim.
The dull light flickers
in rhythm to your shallow breaths

your beating heart.

DEBIT/CREDIT

They say she's a credit card junkie.
But I don't care!

I slop some poetry onto the sidewalk
underneath the awning of my
cash-only establishment,
words spill like sewage into the gutter.

She says *wow, like you're really deep.*

So I take her credit
and watch my uninsured account decline
like so many pennies on the dollar.

That night, I take her tab home with me.
She's appreciative, though.
My interest inflates
like old Federal Reserve Notes.

We regain consciousness in the morning
and with the dubious wisdom
that comes from fucking

I say *sweetie, why don't you move in?*

Three hours later
I've got a mop and a broom
a closet full of clothes

and we're selling my drums
on eBay.

WINDOW STRIKES

Like faked-out birds
we slammed into one-another's reflections,
passed out on kitchen linoleum
and drooled until morning sun
split our heads awake.

We paid penance of instant coffee
laced with bourbon
and pancake batter browned in beer,
pretended to job hunt the classifieds
of yesterday's stolen paper,
disconnected phone calls
to end the breakfast charade.

Hair of dog quelling stomach flu
we showered with the passion of young lovers;
became the couple we were meant to be,
tumbling on stained sheets
arching upright against the window,
laughing at the traffic below.

No neighbors would interfere
as the last of our dishes clattered
and our squawking echoed.
Romance only lasted a while
before keeping up with our "Jones"
became the mission,
to score drugs again our only cause
as we blame-gamed one-another
for our sorry-ass condition.

PLASTIC BOTTLE VODKA

Remember when we used to drink plastic-bottled vodka?
That poor-ass supermarket shit.

You walked around the apartment in that torn terrycloth robe
cleavage drooping to the floor

and last night's makeup spattered
like gun powder residue.

I wore the Panama hat inside
because I thought that was really funny,

but my plastic-rimmed glasses were broken,
held together with superglue and scotch tape.

Indifferent to everything,
we routinely ignored the rent.

So the manager would bang on the door every Sunday morning
louder than our heads could complain.

From your open purse you dredged crumpled bills and coin;
I signed over my unemployment check.

When you whined about the hole in the carpet
your tit pointed right at it.

Asked to fix the garbage disposal,
the guy would back out the door laughing.

MEMORY PRESERVED IN A
BLUE CERAMIC ASHTRAY

Last time I saw you
we sat in our favorite
shoreline restaurant
underneath sporadic
formations of seabirds.

You broke a blue
lacquered fingernail
smashing out your
Marlboro Light
while cursing me.

The maitre d' called
a cab for you.
I finished my Chivas rocks
paid the check
and left alone.

Sundown rested
behind shark-filled waters.
Headlights animated
hedges and mile markers
on the bleak highway
edging the ocean cliffs
of Malibu.

In my Spanish-tiled flat
under the Mexican Fan Palms
of Venice
sleep came easily
closing my eyes
on your final image:

Red-stained cigarette butt
grainy gray ash
blue ceramic ashtray.

THE LAST SITTING

Bert Stern impressed
my need to mate
a woman like
Marilyn Monroe
when he photographed
the dream angel
of mid-20th Century America
in bed sheets of sensual mayhem
and the silk of a pastel screen
over the rose
of Norma Jean's
forbidden
nipples.

FATHER'S DAY

Climbing up the slide
and down its stairs,
buzzing children
chant half-songs and whines.
They play while I lie,
            eyes sandpapered raw
stubble cheeks
shirt stains.

I dreamt of the cold sea,
milky stars above
black depths,
floes and bergs.
I scraped ice crystals off the bow
ice flaked on black water.
Nose cold, I drop my oars,
my teeth clenched under bitter sky
a child's tune chimes too loud.

The parents wince at my
depression on the grass,
they pull their children away from me.
On top of the slide
a four-year-old girl calls
"King of the hill!"

I lift up my body
to be her father.

4. REENTRY

"Deeper into my forest, I start to understand solitude."

DARK SWIRLING SKY
SHADOWS A WORN-OUT BARN
ON AN UNTRIED ROAD

The skies blacken and eddy
like fumes from a tractor's
blown gasket.
Winds yammer
through paint-chipped slack-boards.
Glacial drafts chill
the long-standing bones
of a once useful structure.

Hailstones drum a felt hat.
Mulching leaves mottle
worn boots.
A ghostly figure seeks warmth
from a swig of Jim Beam
and a nose wipe on the sleeve.

A wet thumb reaches into frame
an 18-wheeler thunders
onto the slick highway
to offer a warm cab and coffee breath,
country classics and a promise:

Beyond the regret of a wrong turn
or neglected barns,
wheat will sway like yellow hair
in a long-abandoned lover's dream.

CALIFORNIA JUNE GLOOM:
IN SOUTH DAKOTA THEY WAIT FOR WEATHER

The gray thickness drowns me
like a dreadful recollection of blunders
            and malapropisms.
It keeps me under morning covers too long
without the advantage of a Sunday aubade.

A midmorning drive, it could be dawn,
wiper blades smear mist across the windshield.
I remember a frightening drive through the lightning storms
of South Dakota,
mystic sizzles and flashes
on the dashboard of my SUV,
electric white spirituality
as hail pellets drum my roof.

In that region weather makes a statement,
unlike the weighty layer of atmosphere
that clouds my home.

In Los Angeles, I hope for a quick wind to purge
the summer's soggy air.

Hills will smell musty
of weed and dirt
short-pant hikers
will wipe their brows with the back of their hand
slap at mosquitoes
and fatigue from the stretch.

Heated winds propel me
along burning streets
and braze my skin like reddened
charcoal. Through the sting of Southern California
vapor I long to be
in the turbulent thundershower
of a South Dakota squall line,
a fresh breath of supernatural power
and perhaps,
resurrection.

RE-ENTRY

A blast of Jasmine blesses the driveway.
My ride torques down for the evening.

Too many thought bubbles
collide into my peace surrender.

I close the door and guard myself
from daytime's danger.

The ottoman absorbs my heat.
I grab the remote control of universal distraction.

Light-fractals 3D my eyes, destroys equilibrium
and hyperventilates my reverie.

WHILE WALKING THE DOG
LAST EVENING

I saw a falling star,
its tail so long,
its head so black,
surely it must rest this morning
in a neighbor's backyard.
Blackened rock, warm to the touch
conspicuous on a thick bed
of blue grass.

If it struck like the truth
it could be the famous boson.
If it had not been honest,
the prayers of many
would nod as they hold on to tomorrow,
while the rest of us scramble
to keep the day intact.

Sometimes, what is visible in the black,
like reflected branches
and multi-galaxies of matter,
would support belief in substance,
while to others
the flickering sky expresses
the divine.

ONCE A FROZEN LANDSCAPE

Cloud-beaten
        skies
cover the bareness of chalky tree limbs
    mulching leaves, snow
           drifts
   rivers iced.

  Brittle icicles crack
        days become dark, long
          and numbered.

A whisky chug breaks
    phlegm, disheartened hack
    of dread settles
        in cyan sunset
      ankles breach sludge,
   staggering footsteps
      trudge.

A rough-hewn shack
    parked in the distance,
      rough-coat
   shingles protect
     injured shoulders
        from falling winter.

In unnerving silence
   embers of a cast-iron stove
    deliver warmth
    to the stalled pilgrim,
     not home yet,
      but safe.

I AM WAITING

AFTER LAWRENCE FERLINGHETTI

I am waiting for my case to come up
for my faults to be judged
and my defects to be banished.
I am waiting for rancor to be dislodged
from the throats of those
who distrust me.
I am waiting for those who defend me
to be absolved of complicity.

I am waiting for moral hazard
to boomerang at the masters
of conceit who fail to protect
the needy.
I am waiting for my collusion
to be pardoned and for my
unwitting membership
to be excised from the Pharisees
who gather to perpetrate deceit.

I am waiting for my defense
to rise against false accusers
and for the disingenuous to drown
in the waters of Noah.

I am waiting for my dreams to not
defeat me
and for my neighbor
to not shun me.
I am waiting for a daughter's embrace,
or a placebo pill,
to mitigate the pain of guilt.

LEXICON

My Dream of Words

At war in the cerebral forest
idioms explode into shrapnel,
words clash with branches,
small-legged animals dodge punctuation
and break ranks as the ground opens

to swallow the ash of my wounded rhyme.
I stand naked at the window,
watch letters build
into well-dressed phrases
and attack like arrows.
I have not the muscle
to counter this assault.

I have become an old man
curled over rough-hewn tables,
who scratches rambling verse onto yellow tablets,
each stroke chafing wits
like abrasions on my mind.

In the cold, my speech freezes,
my blue winter skin jackets the forest trees,
I wrinkle and harden with the bark.

IN CASE OF CRITICISM

Let all the air
out of your lungs.

Let a Spanish Guitar
arpeggio from your head.
Let it counter-beat the voice
that assails you.

Scribble on paper.

Make eye contact
to show that you care.

Nod as if to agree.

Rock on your feet.
Pretend you are on a yacht.
Make a mental grocery list.

Don't look at your watch.

Think about Gina Lollabridgida.

Envision butterflies
surrounding any person
who passes judgment.

THE HIGHWAY IS A BREEZE,
THE FOREST IS A CAVE

Forward light dims to cyan opacity,
Cypress and ferns act as road markers,
faded medians blotch the interstate.
In the rearview mirror, sunset highlights ochre patterns
—light poles, branches and looming headlamps.
As if to accentuate the plodding tempo of my escape
a primer-gray pickup flashes high beams
and scoots into the oncoming lane.

The Studebaker Transtar vanishes around a darkened forest curve
leaving swoosh of charcoal dust to unravel like braids of hair.
Signage reveals "No services for sixty-two miles."
Fuel needle points north, I check my backpack for sustenance.
Dense pines are canyon walls, black and creepy,
my headlights swathe the path of scattered bark.
The road's imbalance guides me like my last waltz,
bald tires sway high to the left, low to the right.

Radio signal loses to static, engine torques against the grade,
wheels thump unseen hurdles on the straightaway,
potholes break rhythm like varied thoughts of gloom.
White knuckles grip the wheel.
Complete darkness. My vehicle motions
through its own misty beam. Cabin dims,
orange dashboard digits glow,
shadows black on drab.

Deeper into my forest, I start to understand solitude,
black pushes against windows, green-eyed memories reflect.
I absorb into the vinyl glass travel vortex.
Raven-hair dreams persist; I look for a focal point,
trying to make out any horizon through shallow field of vision
in the foggy glow of unkempt asphalt.
My pedal pressure continues steady on the floorboard.

JUST BEFORE DAWN

We will drive to a mountain
when the sun is not quite new
wake the sleeping mess of undergrowth
clog our tires on dusty trails
and stall.

Turn out all sounds
silence will conjure muted furs and scales
where hedgerows comfort hibernators.
In the morning's quiet pallor
we make acquaintance.

Berries and needles
spice the skies of turning days,
winds blow past the moist bark
of thick trees that stand in protection,
leaves graze our vehicle
and you are as smart
as the surviving bugs.

We will open the door
walk the path of backdrop
painted for our stay.
We find a stream,
kick our shoes.
A kiss becomes necessary
as your beauty exceeds
fine strokes on wildflowers.

I will touch you
as though I have never held
any Evening Primrose
or looked at orange mottled pebbles
swathed by a cold mountain stream
or felt a rising sun
warm my wintered cheek.

THREE HOLIDAY STARS

Pinholes of billion mile stars
glimmer on Yucca, Palm and Manzanita,
    road gravel kicks the undercarriage
    of a passing van
while innocent voices sing *Carol of the Bells.*
    Star-shine illuminates three little hands
waving in the milky glow
    of a Christian sky.

Because they don't know
    if they are Christian, Muslim or Zen,
glory becomes their very own design,
    without trepidations of the parental fall.
Comet trails direct passage to their joyful night,
    a journey to proclaim holiness
        with scrubbed faces
            and starry eyes of countenance.

    Day breaks on a New Year.
The scornful world evaporates with their colors of joy.
    Three worthy girls learning *Auld Lang Syne*
        in the dryness of Saguaro and sand.

HOW TO BURY YOUR DAD

To my daughters

Find yourself a yellow '67 Volkswagen
with overheating pistons;
call it your "V dub ya bug."
It will burn plenty of fluid.

Careful not to double-clutch
that steep, winding grade
from Santa Rosa to Trinidad.
Enter the fabled shading
of ocean trees
where scents of decomposing air,
old foliage and a bear's
organic spray saturate
the Redwood bark.

Don't fret traveling-day doldrums.
When you tire of driving,
pull off to the side of the road,
let the Humboldt runoff
mottle your boots.
Eat coarse salami, crusty bread
and cheddar cheese.
Your front trunk should carry laundry,
oranges and a red & blue cooler
full of Budweiser and Perrier.

If the fuel line chokes
find a traveling neighbor
to push downhill
until torque overcomes stall.

Soon you'll get to a downgrade clearing
with glimpses of Pacific Ocean
through burley Redwood Goliaths.
Seek a wooded rise
where clouds and mountain peaks are level,
stop and smoke a reefer among the ferns.

When the road levels,
dust my ashes, your geezer dad,
into pine needles and sod;
litter the Avenue of Giants
with my remains.

Rest.

Then carry on to Meyer's Flat, Scotia, Rio Dell,
those peculiar forest towns leading toward Eureka bay.

Experience oil fogged air, northern kelp
and beach salt.
Take a sight seers' dalliance,
travel for days,
watch whales grace the depths
and pelicans claiming bays.

Be sisters, be friends.

Ride that rainy northerly jaunt
through haze and drizzle
'til your wipers fail.

ABOUT THE AUTHOR

Jerry Garcia is a poet, photographer and filmmaker from Los Angeles, California. His poetry has been seen in various journals and anthologies including *Wide Awake: Poets of Los Angeles and Beyond, Coiled Serpent Anthology, The Chiron Review, Askew* and his chapbook *Hitchhiking with the Guilty*. Jerry is a past director of the Valley Contemporary Poets and former President of Beyond Baroque's board of trustees in Venice, California. He has also been a producer and editor of television commercials, documentaries and motion picture previews. Jerry lives with his wife Becky and their poetic dog Japhy.

www.gratefulnotdead.com

Connect With Jerry Garcia

Visit him online at www.gratefulnotdead.com
Facebook: www.facebook.com/gnd54
LinkedIn: www.linkedin.com/in/jerry-garcia-48552a8
Twitter: www. twitter.com/gnd1954
Instagram: www.instagram.com/gnd54/

OTHER TITLES BY GREEN TARA PRESS

BOOKS

Shortcuts to Mindfulness: 100 Ways to Personal and Spiritual Growth, by Catherine Auman, LMFT

In This Hour, by Sandra Sloss Giedeman

Journaling as Sacred Practice: An Act of Extreme Bravery, by Cynthia Gregory

Really Truly, by Holly Prado

Rim of the World Highway, by Margaret Walsh

FOR BEHAVIORAL HEALTH PROFESSIONALS:

Managed Care: A Guide for Behavioral Health Practitioners, by Catherine Auman, LMFT

RELAXATION AND MEDITATION AUDIOS

Awareness Breathing, by Catherine Auman, LMFT

Deeply Relaxed, by Catherine Auman, LMFT

www.ingramcontent.com/pod-product-compliance
Lightning Source LLC
Chambersburg PA
CBHW071617040426
42452CB00009B/1372